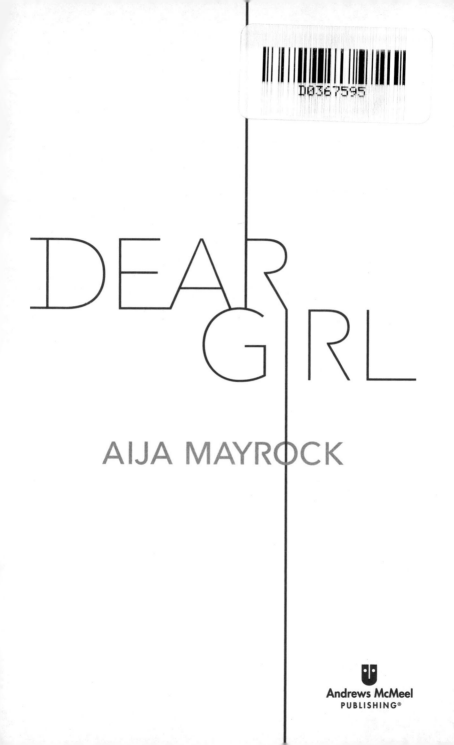

DEAR GIRL

AIJA MAYROCK

Andrews McMeel
PUBLISHING®

DEAR GIRL is a journey from girlhood to
womanhood through poetry
It is the search for truth in silence
The freeing of the tongue
It is deep wounds and deep healing
And the resilience that lies within us
It is a love letter to the sisterhood

A note from the poet: DEAR GIRL is comprised of poetry that is sometimes personal and sometimes cries from the collective. DEAR GIRL is not a memoir, but rather an exploration of the inherent resilience we all share.

THE SEARCH FOR TRUTH IN SILENCE | 1

THE FREEING OF THE TONGUE | 19

DEEP WOUNDS, DEEP HEALING | 41

WITH LOVE | 59

TO THE SISTERHOOD | 81

The words that pour from my lips now
come from lips that were sealed
far too many years.

Drown the world in what they do not wish to hear.
That which they do not wish to hear
is truth.

THE SEARCH
FOR TRUTH
IN SILENCE

In the quiet of the night
I hear my story.
Not my thoughts,
my truth.
The tethers to my ancestors,
the silk web to my future children.
I hear my birth and my death;
I hear my story
and I realize
it's not just my story—
it's the story of the ages.

How we walk gently between
now and eternity.

Dear Girl,

you ask me what I wish for you.
I simply say—
never allow any soul to clip your wings
you were not born an ember,
you were born the flame.

I come from a line of wild women
divine in their pursuit of truth.
For the women I come from
do not run with the wolves;
they lead the pack.

Dear Girl,

oftentimes we women start to rise,
then certain people devise a plan to disenfranchise.

Whether it's our bodies or rights,
entice us with movements,
unite us through persecution.

Dear Girl,
open your eyes.

We have come so far it's easy to resign.
We've got "equality"
but public policy shows the contrary, honestly.
One in six women could be raped in their lives
and it's mostly seen as a victimless crime.

What should every girl know?

You are not some puppet in a puppet show.
Expose the double standards,
the hypocrisy, the hate.

It is never too late.

This is the moment of girls taking the reins.

It is Time's Up.

It is Me Too.

It is everyone from me
to you
who has spoken
or stayed silent
but strong.

And for every survivor who speaks
only to be met
with intimidation, investigation, and disbelief:

Dear Girl,
you will be believed.

If not by Senate floors and investigators,
we will hear you, Dear Girl,
we will see you, Dear Girl,
we will stand by you.

For the survivor three thousand miles away or the
        one next door,
you are heard.

Justice will not always prevail
but we will continue to fight
tooth and nail.

You are heard.

So that our sisters and daughters will never be asked,
rather
harassed,
whether they wanted it,
regretted it,
or just forgot.

Believe me,

no one forgot.

* * *

Dear Everyone,

grab ahold of your voice.
It is time to make a choice

to believe survivors
to pay us all the same
to give women of color equal access and opportunity
to protect the safety of trans girls every day.

Make the choice to change the climate,
make the choice not to stay silent.

This is not the era of girls,
this is the future of girls.

I hid my anger for far too long,
buried it in the bowels of my being
and turned it on myself, like a sword to my own neck.

We are taught
anger is ugly.

Dear Girl,
your rage burns bright and when it is felt
it melts into grief, and from that grief
love is born.

There is love so great
it's like the sun kissing the sea goodnight
as it melts into the horizon.

That love
is a mother's love.

Dear Mother,

I see your fears baked into how you raised me.
I see them tremble from your lips as you warn me.
I know you are terrified of the world that could swallow
     me whole.
But Mother, you need not fear,
because even if I am swallowed up,
I will kick until I am spit back out.
I will fight with the fists you gave me.
I will shout from the gut you built for me.

Dear Mother,
you need not worry.
For I am the warrior you always dreamed you'd have.
I will not go down fighting
because I will not go down at all.

When a girl is born into a world
where she has no control over her body,
she learns to live in a body that is not hers, but owned
　　　by the state.
She grows up to believe that obedience is her middle name.

When a girl is born into a world
that does not value her body,
she learns to exist on the periphery of society
as if growing into her spine is too much to ask for.

Your cruelty is no match for my spirit.
Try to break me
and you will see
love that pours like blood from my wounds.
To break me, you would have to make me hate,
and like I said,
your cruelty is no match for my spirit.

You tell your daughter that she is being emotional, irrational,
yet you tell your son that he is being strong, smart;

you are teaching your daughter to doubt her feelings,
to question her beliefs.

And so when she is mistreated,
she will think back to what was said
under your roof
and believe those gut feelings we speak of
are merely irrational thoughts,

while your son believes every thought he has is fair and right.

Be careful how you raise your daughters.
Be careful how you raise your sons.

When you teach your daughter
that her body is only pure untouched,
you are teaching her
that she can be ruined at the hand of man.
Raise your daughter to know
that what's in between her thighs
is hers to own,
whether it be for a woman, man, or anyone to see.
Teach your daughter
that she is a gift
so she knows her worth
but doesn't feel shame
in sharing her beauty.

Dear Girl,

there is a fire raging inside of you;
do not allow anyone to try to extinguish it:
it is mighty
it is brave
it is you.

And so on those nights
when you think you are broken,
remember the flame
and feel it burn.

Next time they are cruel to you,
listen carefully,
and if you listen
you will hear their pain,
and just like that
you will see their heart.

I don't know what I'm doing;
all that I do know is
I chase what sets my soul on fire
to the ends of earth,
till the end of time.

When you are lost,
look back at the women you came from,
for they were warriors
and their path
will guide you
to yours.

THE FREEING
OF THE TONGUE

She has a fire that you can see when you look into her eyes,
flames swallow up her self doubt.
She always runs toward the storm;
nothing scares her more than turning down a challenge,
nothing scares her more than taping down her wicked tongue.

Bullied and brutalized for my stutter and lisp, for years
    I did not speak.
One day, I untaped my own wicked tongue.
Letting words climb the rungs of my vocal chords,
    I began to tell my story.
And I watched their faces in awe as they said to me:

"You are not who we thought you'd be."

I am the woman I am today
because my father never clipped my wings,
even in disagreement.
I hear his voice,
all pride and no shame, say—

"And, yes, that is my daughter."

And so I soar.
I soar.
I soar.

Dear Girl,

I wish I could hold you and say
the world will protect you.
But I know it will not,
and in some way,
you, too, know it will not.

Maybe that's why when people tell you,
"You're too young to understand,"
you smirk with that twinkle in your eye.

Because the moment you were born,
you were sexualized, objectified,
power never recognized.

Dear Girl,
I know that if this world harms you,
attempts to break you,
you will rise
broken and bruised.
The world is no match
for that flame in your eyes.

This is for all the women who have lived according to
    the male gaze,
who have been slut-shamed,
who have been trained to fear the dark alleyways,
who have been taught that "No" is not a complete sentence,
that it's in the "male DNA",
that accountability is just getting carried away,
that boys will be boys even when they know the difference.

This is for all the women:

do not shrink into that corner,
do not cover your body in shame,
do not silence your own voice
in a revolution that has only just begun.

Raise your daughters like you raise your sons;
the inequality did not begin with her birth,
the inequality begins when you choose to raise
     your daughter in a box labeled "ladylike"
and your son, in no box, with no label.

When told
your dress begets savagery,
I hope you respond,
"Then it fits me perfectly."

You savage girl.

Giving girls and women the decision
to take control of their bodies
is equality.

Equality is having access to contraception
with no exception, no stigmatized perception;

a day when women are taught
that their sexuality need not be hidden,

boys are given condoms in high school
while girls are taught to live under a different set of rules—

rules that encourage purity and modesty,
a monopoly on a woman's body.

I refuse to be ashamed
of the fact
that my body does bleed each month;
it is why we are all here,
and for that
I will not tuck
my tampons into my sleeve
as I scurry to the bathroom.
It really is no secret
that we bleed.

There is a world up ahead
where people are not targeted
for beliefs or bodies
where peace isn't fantasy,
it's reality.

Build the world you hope your children will see.

There is no such thing as weak women,
only women
who have not stepped into
their power.

Step into it.
The world is waiting.

You were not born to please,
you were brought here to
disrupt, awaken, and speak truth,
to ease the pain scattered around
and so when you are told to quiet down,
I hope you grow louder.
You are an entire symphony
that needs no applause.

When you are knocked down,
remember
it's not what made you fall,
it's what makes you
get back up.

No good revolution came from
safety and security;
revolution begins when you leap into the unknown
and shout from the rooftops:

I am here. Alone or surrounded by thousands. I am here.
    And I am not going anywhere.

The Truth about Being a Girl

People always say that the girls of this generation are
        so vain:
"Why can't they put their brains toward books instead
        of good looks?"

I used to blame girls too: "Be more than a perfect body
        and a pretty hairdo."

But then I stepped into the world
and opened my eyes to the truth about being a girl.

I heard guys say things like, "Dude, she was tighter than
        that girl you hit and quit."
or
"I wanna pipe your sister someday."
or
"Her ass looks like a racetrack with those stretch marks,
        but at least it's big like Kim K's."

I never grew up thinking of those things.
Don't blame me, but when I thought about boys,
I thought about dinner dates and soul mates,
not fuckbois that look at you like shark bait.

It breaks my heart for every girl growing up in this world.

Instead of "How was your day?" messages,
we get, "You up? Wanna come fuck?"

I am not an object.
I have a voice and something to say.

Do not assume that I belong in your bedroom.
I belong in a conference room.

And for anyone who thinks that this generation is so vain,
it's because we girls are held under a microscope day
  after day.

* * *

It's like
"beautiful" doesn't even exist
unless you can cross everything off the checklist:

big butt
big boobs
skinny waist

Includes:
small nose
plump lips
bony hips

Hairless,
careless,
but still has an awareness.

In all fairness,
I want to be seen as beautiful too.

I mean,
I don't want to be demeaned.

I mean,
I am not the same girl I was at fifteen.

I mean,
I am stuck in between
being a girl and a woman.

Growing up in a world
that has taught me to look sexy,
get a degree,
maybe a little rhinoplasty,
but never,
never
disagree with misogyny.

A world that has taught me
that being a woman
means living in fear
that your basic health care
will disappear,

or
that your paycheck
might somehow be smaller
than a man
who does the same job,

or
that your boss will tell you to stop giving him
eyes
"If you want a raise, you gotta compromise.
Show me what lies above those thighs."

Boy, please.

The moment you misidentified everything,
you forgot
that a hundred years ago
I could not vote.

Look at what happens
when you try to demote
the very bodies
that give birth to you.

Please.

We are used to it all
and we are appalled
but, you see,
we don't know what it's like to be free.

* * *

Equality
is not just about
calling someone out.

Equality is accountability.

It is my brother knowing
that I am equal to him.
So equality
is education

from classrooms
and courtrooms,
to conference rooms
and computer screens.

Equality is truth,
is strong voices.

It is breaking through the silence that exists,
because silence
can't exist
if it's not tolerated.

Equality is you
changing the future,
clearing the path

for every woman
and
every man.

It is raising the next generation to know
that not only
does their voice matter

but
it will be heard.

We have the power in our hands.
As we will not sit back
and nod
and smile
while certain people

reconcile
the rules
of being fertile.

Sorry, but it's my body, baby.

I may be a young lady
but my father always taught me
to speak out
and fight
against injustice of every kind.

We will not stop
until we hold our rights
for women of every color
size
shape
sexual identity
and place
in this world.

And that is the truth about being a girl.

If you don't set your spirit free now
then when
will you
find
your wild?

DEEP WOUNDS, DEEP HEALING

Heal your wounds, Dear Girl,
so your daughter
isn't born
with the same ones.

She does not report her rape
because neither did her mother or grandmother;
in fact, they did not call it rape
they called it sex
and sometimes love.

She does not report her rape
because she has never been taught
that her body has value
and her voice has worth.

She drinks to soothe the pain
that lived in her mother's heart.
As much as we might hope,
we are not so different from our mothers.

Her pain
is my pain,
and my pain
is my daughter's.

To break the chain of trauma
heals a constellation of wounds.

They do not speak about the tragedies that have come
        and gone from their four walls.
As if silence is more palatable
then the words that need to be spit.

In silence, there is trauma,
legacy passed down from seed to embryo to the first beat of
a heart.

To break the chain of anger
you need not bear it
on the back
your mother built for you.

She tears down others
because, since birth,
she was taught
to tear down herself.

To get through it,
you must go through it,
and yes
it will hurt,
but you—
you will survive.

Split open your wounds for me,
I know how to heal them.
One silky word spills from my lips,
I know how to heal them.

I have healed my own.
I have cut them open
just to know they were real.
And I have sewn them up
just to know I could.

If you feel consumed by your trauma,
seek healing.
For I once believed
I could never let go
of my demons,
and now I live with them,
trailing behind,
visiting them when I want
but only when I want.

How do you bear
what you cannot bear
so beautifully
it makes it look easy?

At my most broken,
I saw beauty
in just one thing:

looking at the pieces of myself
scattered and shattered,
I wanted to be put back together.

Dear Boy,

when you touch her, remember your power
to love or to break.
When you touch her, remember you may watch porn, but
you are not in it.
When you touch her, remember her body was born from a
mother like yours.

Dear Boy,
your hands leave imprints,
visible or not.
Remember your power to love or to break.

We all have a shadow side,
I just never knew
his was so dark.

I am still guilty of fighting my body
to fit a standard of beauty
that is attainable only with
surgery and starvation,
and yet
it's a battle
I can't seem to stop fighting.

Cruelty comes from our very own wounds.

You might believe the words you speak are weak,
but the echoes of words
can start revolutions.

Use your words to mend—
you and you alone
hold all of that power.

Growing up,
the world taught me
that vulnerability should be a secret.

I grew up believing
that the hero of a story
never showed signs of weakness.
I disguised my demons
so there was no sign of struggle.

My vulnerability is not my weakness;
it is my superpower.
I wear it like a cape
and watch mouths gape
at the sight of
a warrior
wearing wounds like crown jewels.

My vulnerability
is more powerful
than wielding a sword
or a shield.

No one teaches us that
resilience rises like a wildfire
from pain.

The battles you fight do not take away
from who you are.

Dare to teach the world
that weakness doesn't exist.
Weakness
is just a seed
that no one sees
sprouting into genius.
Own your story
like you wrote it
by yourself.

You are the hero.
The hero is imperfect.
Wear those wounds like crown jewels.

You are leading a deeper life now;
it's not one that you've chosen
but it's deeper.

WITH
LOVE

Dear First Love,

when you broke my heart,
it wasn't because you didn't love me anymore.

You broke my heart
because you changed
how I saw myself,

and in that
I've never been more heartbroken.

When I picked up the pieces of my heart,
I saw something much sadder.
You were not the first one to teach me to hate myself.
I was.
And so the work began
of loving myself again
or maybe for the first time.

He knew nothing of my story
or where I'd come from,
but he looked at me
like I was the most fantastic hurricane he had ever seen.

And in that moment I realized
I didn't have to explain.
I had met someone
who could see through me.
I was a window
for the first time in my life.

I'd never felt so naked and afraid.
But I ran toward him,
not away.

I fear you'll leave me
and that is so strange;
I am more whole when you are not here,
yet half full is what I dream of these days.

I ask you to stay
the same way
the sea
begs the shore
for more.

He went from man to giant,
casting a shadow over my life
so much so
I could not see anything but him.

That terrifies me:
how someone,
anyone
can block the light.

And one day
I hope
your path leads you
to a place
where you love yourself
as much as I love you.

Perhaps then
you will understand
how I
and so many others
fell madly
for you.

Leaving someone you love
is like leaving home
and knowing you can never return.

Missing you
is the cruelest thing I could do to my heart,
and maybe that's why I do it:
it's easier to hurt myself
than to love myself.

I rewrite our history
like a novelist,
one sentence at a time
until each chapter is entirely fictionalized.
But, oh, how beautifully it reads.

And sometimes people do change;
still, who they used to be stays sewn in our hearts like
the faintest of scars.
We ask the question—
"Is it really possible to begin again?"

In heartbreak, remember:

You are but one life.
Millions have come before
and millions will come after.

They too
have shared
or will share
the same breaking of the heart
and survived.

When you lose someone you love
look up at the sky,
each day bleeds into night;
just like that
the moon arrives, the stars line the sky
and in mere moments
the night evaporates
into sunrise.

Ending and beginning
in darkness and in light,

that is the cycle
of this very life.

Dear Child,

I will not shame you for loving who you love.
Your magic is your untamed spirit.
Shame bleeds through
generation to generation;
that is not the legacy
I wish for you.
Even in culture and decade divides
I dream a life of love for you,
child of mine.

"What if there is not enough time?" the adult asked.
"Why is right now not enough?" the child responded.

Each time I fall back into my fifteen-year-old mind
I stand on my grown feet,
look into my grown eyes,
and remind myself—

"You are alive. Not for nothing. You are alive."

I had all of the love in the world
but I could not see it.
We are blind
when we don't know how
to love the very bones
and blood
that make us.

Peer into the depths of your soul
and see—
your magic exceeds that of the stars.
Imagine you are viewing the universe.
You are.

It is possible
for two hearts
to be sewn together,
bound
across borders and seas;
that heart
is a father's heart
melting open
the first time he sees
his daughter.

Dear Brother,

you hold my secrets
like they are diamonds
and my trust like gold;

our hearts are woven together
as rebel kids
and grown adults.

You ask me what I wish for you.
I simply say,
cling to your inner child
as if childhood
were yesterday.

It would be a tragedy
if you settled for something
less extraordinary
than the magic
you hold.

TO THE
SISTERHOOD

Dear Girl,

I am the sister
you do not know
and will never meet,

but I am your sister
nonetheless.

Dear Sisters,

my whole life I've struggled
with trusting women.

I heard girls say things like,
"I love her, but she's a dirty ho."
"She'd be so much prettier without that nose."
"She's not that talented; she'll never make it.
        Think of the ratio."

These are your sisters.
We don't exist in silos.

I propose we outgrow
our opposition to one another.
Our experience
is of each other.

If we're fighting for equality,
there has to be camaraderie.

This is a letter
to every woman
who knows better
than to scarlet-letter,
to whisper
and backstab
a sister.
There is no progress
when we march
in different directions.

Correction:
there is no progress
when we march
in discriminatory sections.

White women,
show up
for your sisters of color.

Straight women,
show up
for your lgbtq+ sisters.

Women,
show up,
have the guts
to overlook differences,
because really
the difference is
as drastic as
progress
or
no progress.

We can't afford to divide each other.
Since early days
we are taught
to compare and compete
with one another.

You are not devalued
even if
the woman next to you
appears to be perfect.

You are not devalued
if your sisters
are achieving
greatness.

You are always of value
if you
value
you.

Dear Sisters,

hold yourselves accountable.

Show up for those
you might not know
or understand.

Show up for those
you might not
like at all.
Show up for all of us.

I am sorry that the world
has taught you that
beauty is white and thin.

I'm sorry that the world
has taught you
that your thighs
are not supposed to kiss
as if they were lovers' lips

or that your hair
is supposed to be waxed
or clipped
as if
your body
were someone else's lawn.

I will be there for you
through your darkest days,
I will stand with you
through the most painful decisions.
That is what makes me your sister:
it is not blood,
it's thicker.

When you fall,
I will brush the dirt from your knees
and see you off
toward your
next
great adventure.

Your past lives with you, Dear Girl,
but you
are not your past.

If you want to fly,
you must let go
of all that weighs you down.

You are nowhere near the end of your story—
your story has just begun to write itself.

Let go of perfection—
it doesn't exist.

Let go of your demons—
they are not welcome here.

Let go of your trauma—
you can live with it,
but you need not live in it.

Let go of wanting to go back—
there is no going back,
there is only going forward,
and forward
is more extraordinary
than you could ever imagine.
There is even something beyond the horizon.

Inadequate is not how anyone would describe you—
don't you dare label yourself
as such.

Dear Sister,

I will never judge you for staying.
You know best
how to care
for your wounded parts.
I only hope you follow
the voice
that tells you
when it's time
to go.

You are that which
chases the storm
but sleeps through a beautiful day;
you have broken the hearts of those who loved you
and you have broken your own heart over those who don't.
You never learn
and you laugh when they tell you, "It's time to grow up."
They don't know what you know, Dear Girl:
grow wiser, grow deeper, but never grow up.

For all the women whose stories have been told,
whose voices have echoed,
"Me too."
Thank you.
And for all the women whose voices will never be heard,
we will not forget you.
You are the warriors we seek
when the world turns its cheek.
We will stand in solidarity,
for you are the women we've been waiting for.
Wicked-tongued women
who speak their truths
like a sledgehammer to the glass ceiling,

You are nothing but sheer miracles,
born from the ashes of women
who have walked this earth before you.

That is why you must speak truth,
for other women have done the work
and you must not dismantle it.

Step out of your own shadow.
Step into yourself.
You have come this far
by showing up
with your own two feet
and that alone
is enough.

Her crow's-feet carry seas
and fleets of ship,

sweet words climb
the gruff edges
of her vocal chords,

and they sound rough
as the wildest street corners.

They are remnants
of a life well lived,

the darkly lit moments
between vitality
and the final few words.

I wrote to find the answers,
instead
I found myself.

Be the light
that floods the wounds
of people lost
in their own darkness.

For those
who came here seeking,
I hope you found what you
were looking for.

Aija Mayrock is a poet and writer. Aija's first book, *The Survival Guide to Bullying,* was published in 2015. She graduated from NYU in 2019. This is Aija's debut book of poetry.

Enjoy DEAR GIRL as an audiobook,
wherever audiobooks are sold.

I want to acknowledge all of the hands that carried me here.
For those who picked me up when I fell,
believed in me when I did not believe in myself,
and loved me so deeply and unconditionally.

From the bottom of my heart, I thank you.

DEAR GIRL

Andrews McMeel Publishing
a division of Andrews McMeel Universal
1130 Walnut Street, Kansas City, Missouri 64106

www.andrewsmcmeel.com

www.aijamayrock.com

20 21 22 23 24 BVG 10 9 8 7 6 5 4 3 2 1

ISBN: 9781524856175

Library of Congress Control Number: 2020931364

Editor: Allison Adler
Art Director: Julie Barnes
Production Editor: Meg Daniels
Production Manager: Carol Coe

ATTENTION: SCHOOLS AND BUSINESSES

Andrews McMeel books are available at quantity discounts
with bulk purchase for educational, business, or sales
promotional use. For information, please e-mail the
Andrews McMeel Publishing Special Sales Department:
specialsales@amuniversal.com.